Write your name:

ai

Snake is talking to Bee, but she doesn't hear him. She puts her hand behind her ear and says *ai?* Snake tells her she should say *pardon.*

Action: Cup your hand over your ear as if you are trying to hear something, and say *ai?*

Trace over the dotted lines.

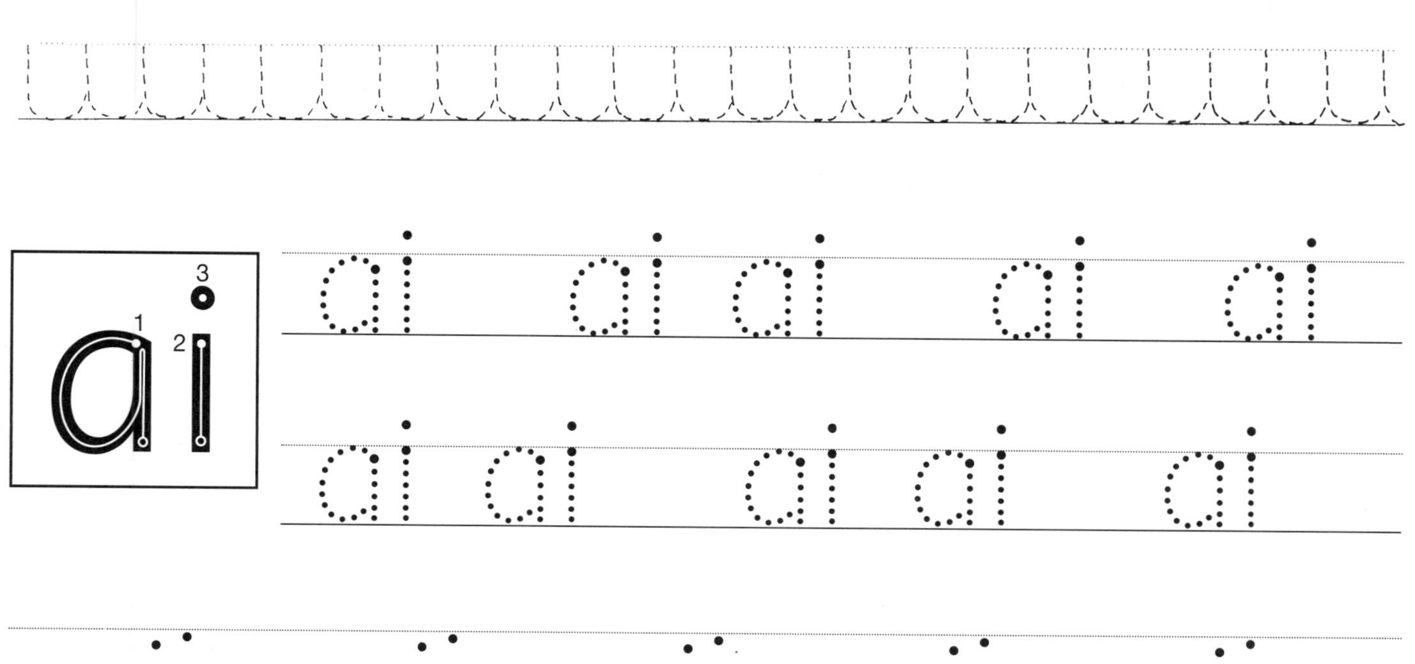

r ai n

t ai l

tr ai n

sn ai l

J j

Snake joins in the fun with Inky and pretends he is wobbling like jello on a plate, saying *j, j, j.*

Action: Pretend to wobble like jello on a plate, saying *j, j, j, j.*

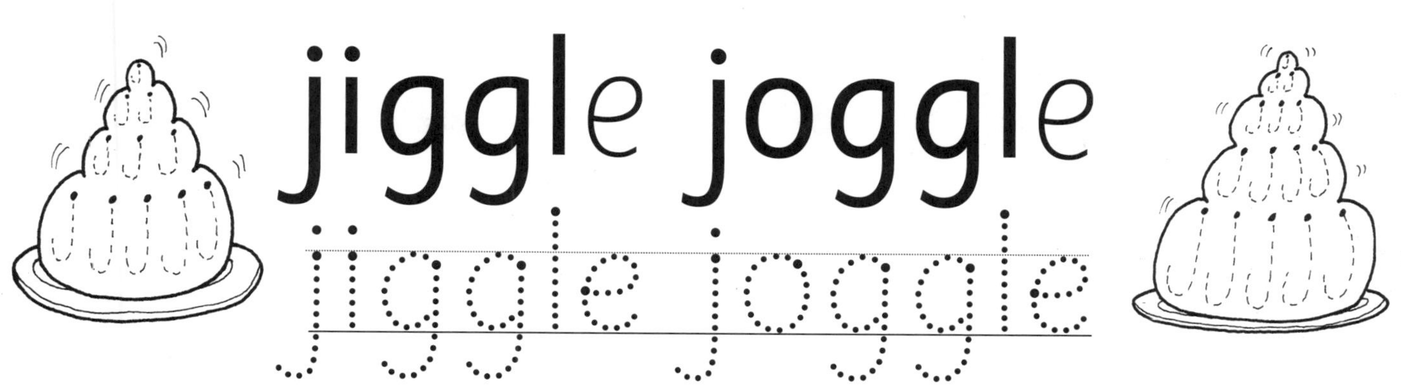

Note: The ‹e› is silent here in "jiggle" and "joggle," so it is shown in faint type.

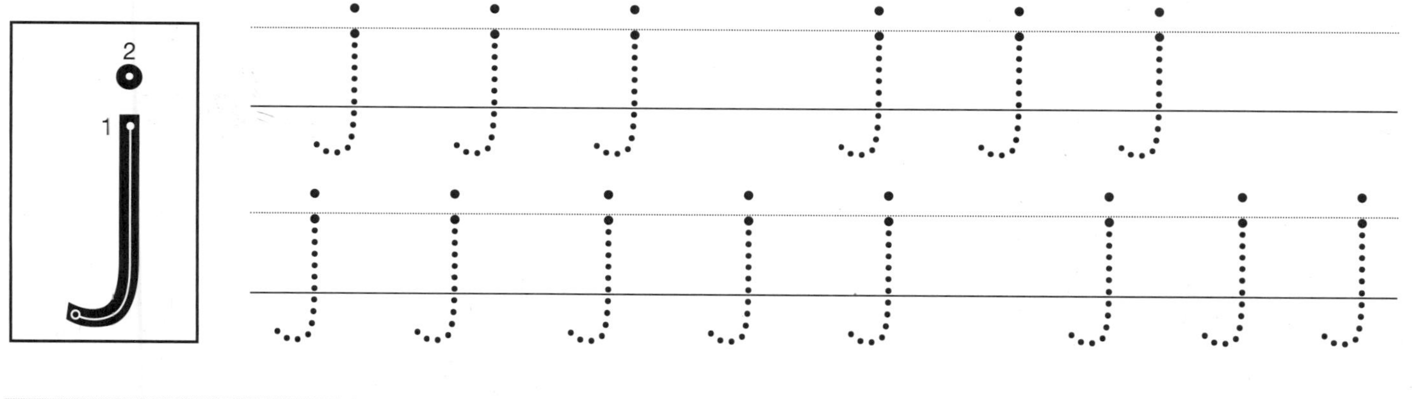

A big oak tree has fallen on the poor old goat. When Bee and Inky see what has happened, they say *oa!*

oa

oa

oa

oa

Action: Bring your hand over your mouth as if something has gone wrong, and say *oa!*

Trace the dotted lines to make the pattern.

ie

A boy is going to a party as a sailor. As he is getting ready, he salutes and says *ie, ie!*

Action: Salute as if you are a sailor, saying *ie-ie.*

Trace over the dotted lines.

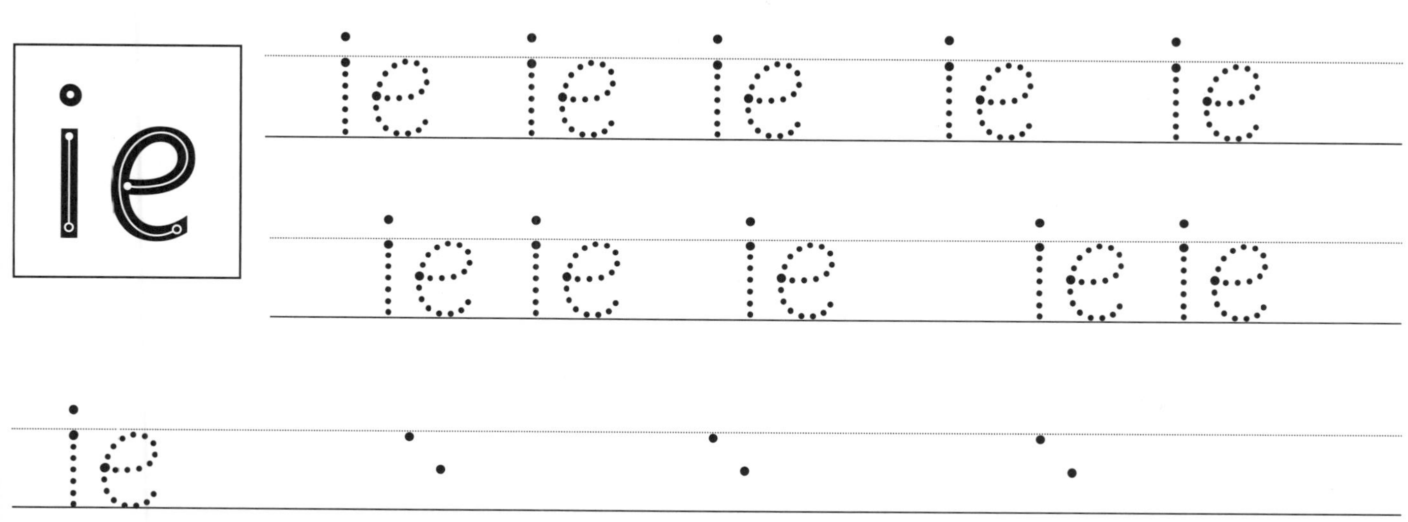

pie

flies

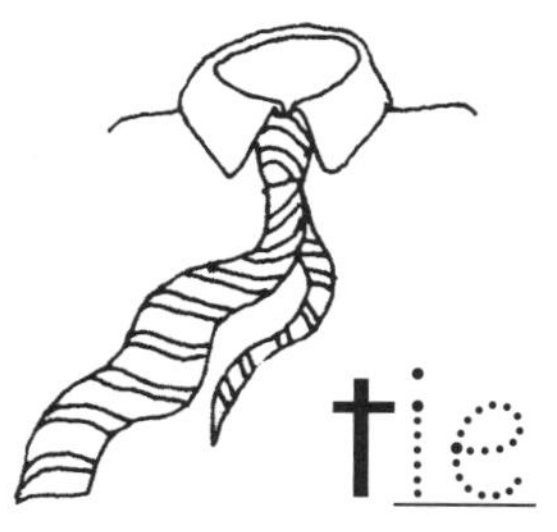

tie

magpie

ee or

Snake and Inky know a very friendly donkey. Whenever he sees anyone, he waggles his ears and calls *ee or! ee or!*

Action: Put your hands on your head like a donkey's ears. Point them up for *ee* and down for *or*.

ee or ee or

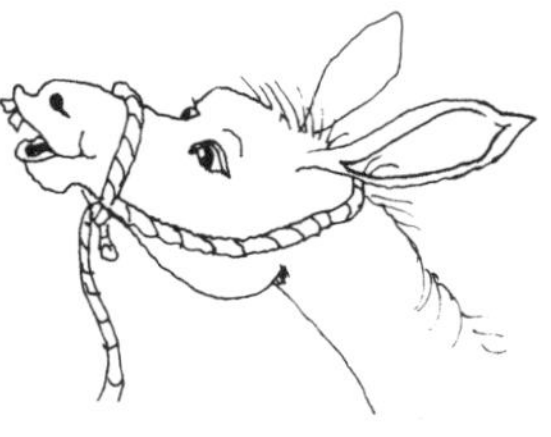

ee

ee ee ee ee ee

ee ee

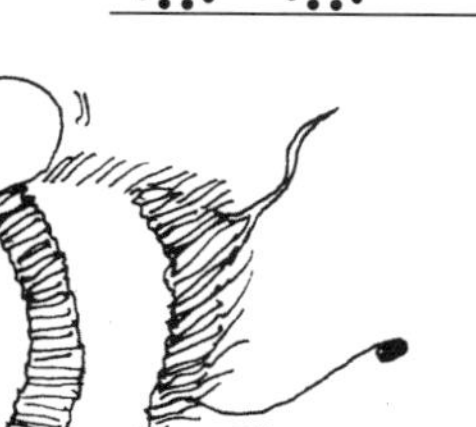

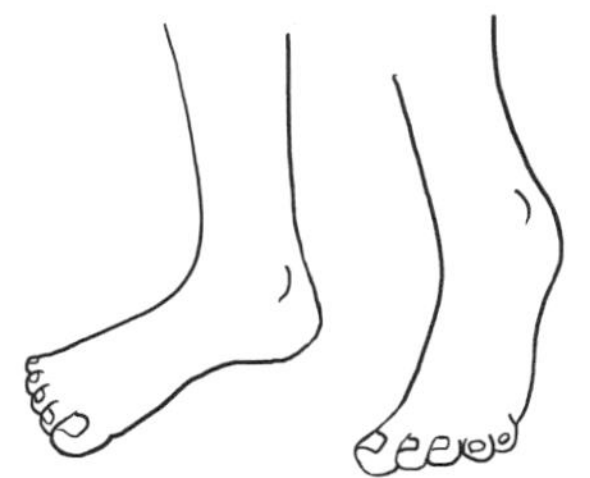

bee feet tree

or

or or or or or

or or

fork

storm horse

Look at each picture and listen for the sounds in the word. Then write the letters for the sounds and read the word.

___ ___ ___

___ ___ ___

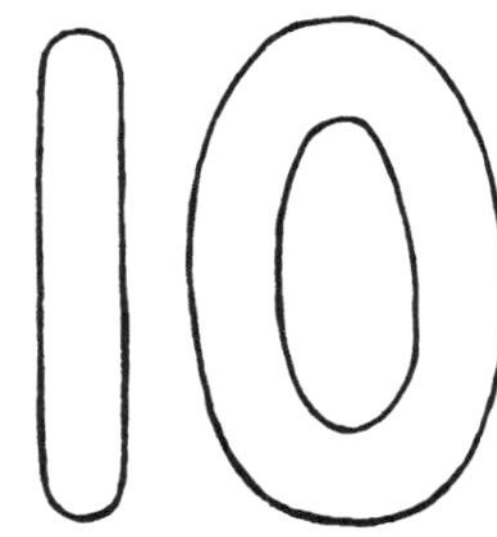

___ ___ ___

___ ___ ___

___ ___ ___

___ ___ ___

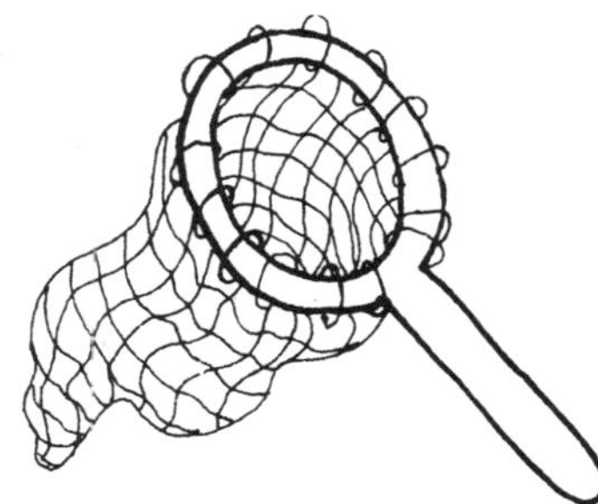

___ ___ ___

___ ___ ___

___ ___ ___

Each dot represents one sound. For each word, point to the dots, say the sounds, and listen for the word. Then draw a picture.

Read the phrases and match each one to its picture.

a big train •

a green frog •

a nest and eggs •

an oak tree •

ducks on a pond •

Anagrams

Say the words, listen for the sounds, and write the words.

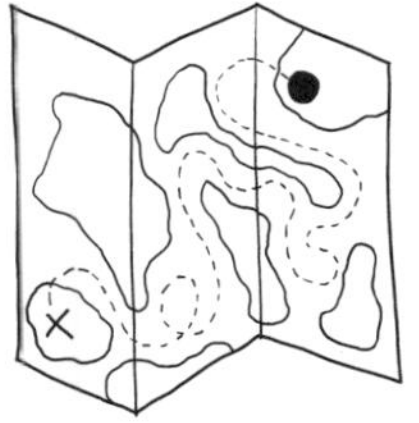

p
m
a

___ ___ ___

o
l
g

___ ___ ___

n
p
e

___ ___ ___

e
n
t
s

___ ___ ___ ___

ll
i
h

___ ___ ___

p
n
o
d

___ ___ ___ ___

ai
r
n

___ ___ ___

r
ee
t

___ ___ ___

t
c
oa

___ ___ ___

Trace over the dotted lines to make the wave patterns in the sea.

Join each picture to its digraph.

Write, read, and draw a picture.

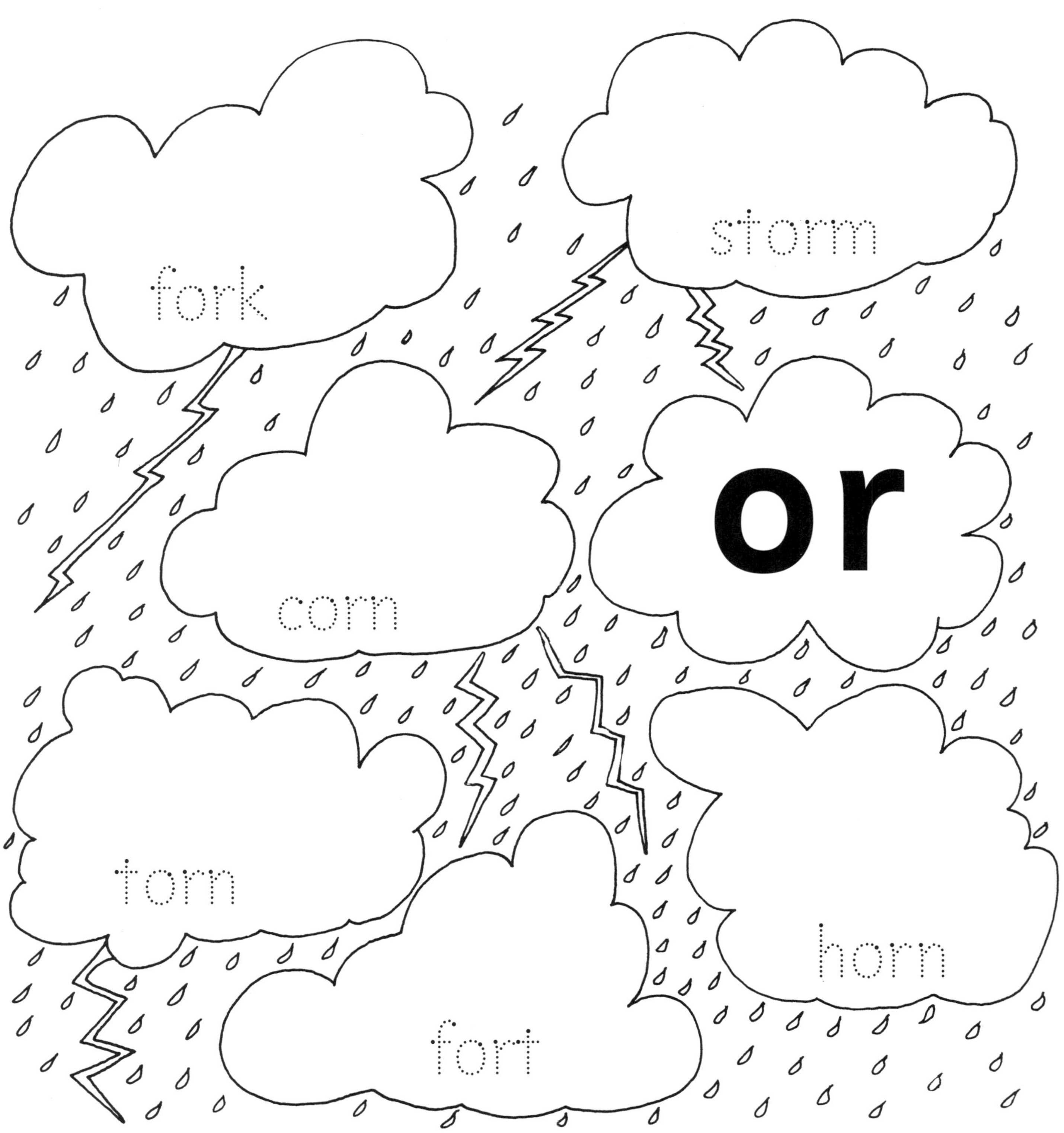

Join each picture to its digraph.

Fill in the letters and read the words.

Read the words, then join each word to its picture.

Say the word for each picture and listen for the sounds. Then write the letters for the sounds and read the word.

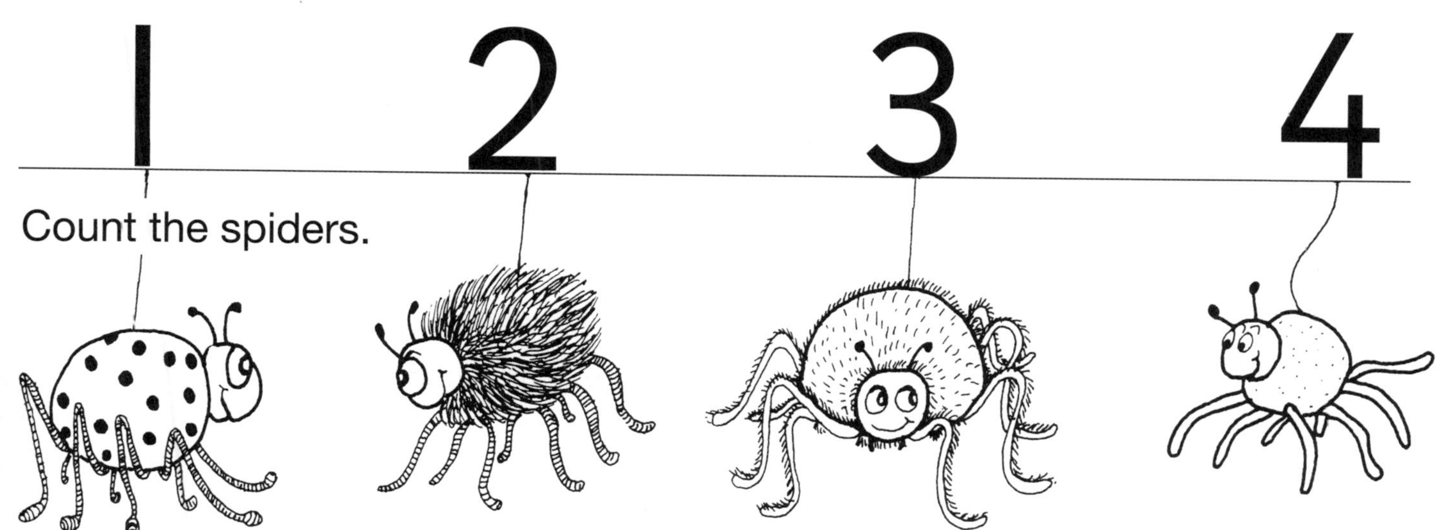

Count the spiders.

Trace over the dotted lines to write the number 4.

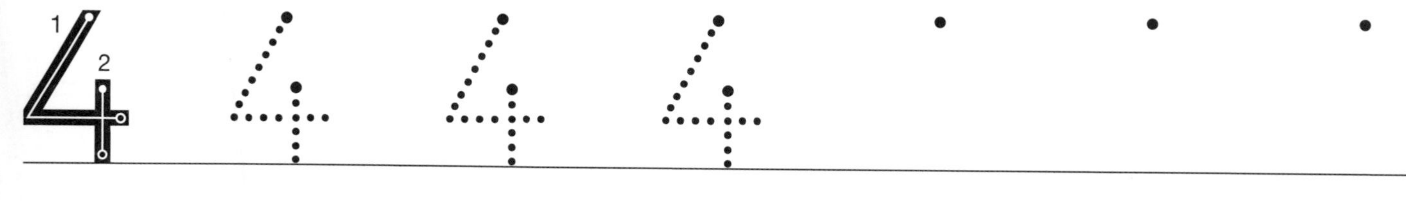

Find the 4 spiders.

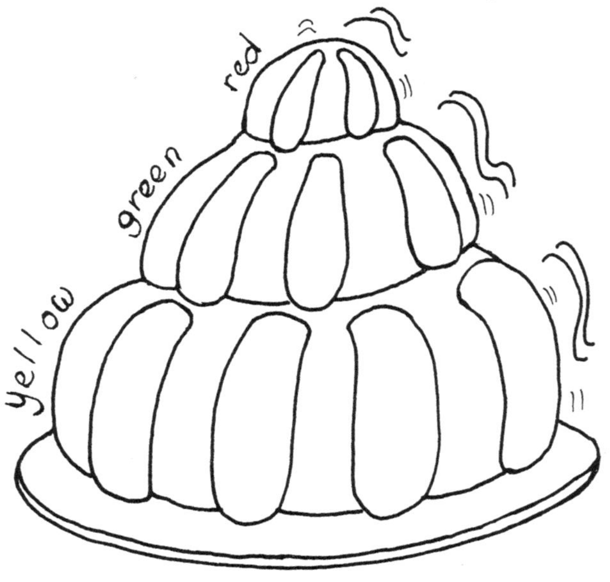

Make some multicolored jello

Make some jello in the first color and leave it to set at the bottom of the mold. Then repeat with two other colors, leaving each color to cool a little before adding it to the mold. When set, turn the jello out, and watch it wobble!

Raindrops

String together some paper raindrops.

Write /ai/ words on them, such as *rain, sail, train, brain.*

Make your own vowel forest

Make a wall poster of the vowel forest. Cut out four big tree shapes and stick them on a large piece of paper. Collect words and pictures that use the long vowel sounds /ai, ee, ie, oa/, and stick them on the correct trees. (Keep a space for the /ue/ tree activity in Workbook 7.)

Play I-Spy

Choose an object you can see and say “I spy, with my little eye, something beginning with /t/” (for example). The others look for things beginning with that sound and guess the answer. Vary the game by saying “something *ending* with....”